Faith Still Works

Faith Still Works

Cover Design by *Audience of One Media*

This book is set in the typeface *Athelas* designed by Veronika Burian and Jose Scaglione.

Paperback ISBN: 9798335109055

Produced in Partnership with *Tall Pine Books*
www.tallpinebooks.com

Please contact the author for further information:
Lovely Louise Reckley | Marsh Harbour, Abaco | Bahamas
Email: louisereckley@gmail.com

| 1 24 24 20 16 02 |

Faith Still Works

Lovely Louise Reckley

*This book is dedicated to my loving husband,
Bradley Reckley, who has been my pillar of strength.*

Contents

Acknowledgments

I thank God for the wonderful relationship that we have and for all the experiences that He has allowed me to have so that I can use them as a testimony to help others.

I would like to thank Malissa McIntosh, who I truly appreciate for all the hard work and countless hours she dedicated towards this project.

Introduction

> "Now faith is the substance of things hoped for, the evidence of things not seen." Hebrews 11:1

Writing has never been my thing but it was not on my mind. One day I heard the voice of the Spirit telling me to write. I didn't know where to start, but God has a time and season for everything. We have to learn how to know the season that we are in where God will connect us to the right person for the season that we are in. I thank God for my sister in Christ, Malissa McIntosh, a woman who wears many hats, and writing is one of those hats. She encouraged me to start writing.

This book is for those who are going through difficult times and feel like they have been forgotten. I want you to know that you are never alone and that God is always with you. When you can't trace Him, He is right there. For some of us who are stretched more than others, the stretching is not about you or for you, but it's for those around you. Whatever God has called you to do, don't procrastinate and stop finding excuses, but just get it done.

You will find that what God has called you to, is what will challenge you. If you are called to a healing ministry, you will have health issues. If your calling is to encourage, you will be discouraged. You have to stay focused. Knowing who you are and Whose you are will keep you going. When you have been called to ministry, you will be tested and tried. There are mountains and valley experiences. We have to remain strong and steadfast. Faith is like our title deed; no matter what we are going through, we have to just hold on to our faith. Without faith, it's impossible to please God. Do we really have faith to believe that whatever we ask for we shall receive? Sometimes, it seems like we are praying in vain. It seems like nothing is working out. It's not by sight or feeling, it's our belief, so whatever we are praying for we have to believe.

Jesus told the disciples that if they had faith the size of a mustard seed, they could speak to the mountain and it would have to move. There are some things that we pray about that we need to speak to. God has given us the power. The Word says that "the same power that raised Jesus from the dead" (see Romans 8:11) is in us. We have to activate our faith for it to work. So many times we allow fear to get the best of us instead of believing the Word of God. We believe what we see in the natural world with our eyes. Instead of living in a place of victory, we live defeated. When we have our faith in God, nothing will shake us because we should be rooted and grounded in God. Our faith is not like a garment that we put on and take off; it's in our hearts. Our faith in God will cause us to be like the three Hebrew boys; nothing and no one will cause us to lose our faith in God. God still honors faith. He honored the faith of the Hebrew boys and protected them, and He will do the same for you.

When Job went through all of his testing, he said, "Though he slay me, yet will I trust in him" (Job 13:15). So many of us live stressed out and as a result of stress, we end up with so many different sicknesses. People die from stress. Most of the sickness that we have comes from stress.

I had to really get to the place where I had to trust God. My life was in turmoil; everything that could go wrong was going wrong. My marriage, my health, my finances were crazy, and I wanted to give up on life. I felt like there was no way out. I was a Christian who loved God, but I felt like I was forgotten. I felt like I was all alone. But I remembered the Word, "I will never forsake you nor leave you in all that we go through." We have to remember the Word. As I look back over my life, I always loved the Lord and wanted to serve Him. I have so much to thank God for. Sometimes we feel like being a Christian excludes us from trouble and problems. Yet we go through them because the enemy is after our faith. If he can get us to doubt God, he has already won. We have to walk according to the Word. We can't walk by what we see. If we walk by sight, it will destroy our walk with God. When trouble comes and it seems like there's no way out, we begin to look at our problems.

When Jesus went to the disciples walking on the waters, they were so afraid. It was not until Jesus spoke that they recognized His voice. Peter called out to Jesus saying, "If it's you, bid me to come." He got out of the boat and began walking on the waters, but all of a sudden, he looked at the waves and listened to the winds. Jesus told him to keep his eyes on him. This is what we have to do in life, keep our eyes on Jesus.

Faith still works is a small collection of the many events that stretched my faith in God. I have experienced many difficult situations where I had no other choice but to trust God. I had to stand in the gap for myself and my family and watch God bring us out victorious. I wrote this book as a reminder to myself of how good God has been to me. As I reflect, I am also encouraged that He will continue to work on my behalf.

As you read the pages of my testimony, it is my prayer that you will be uplifted, encouraged and challenged to continue to walk by faith and not by sight. It is my hope that your faith will be stretched to believe God for others when they don't believe for themselves. This is a part of our mission, to go and tell others that our God is ready, willing and able to heal every disease and to set the captive free. Our God is still in the healing and deliverance business, and it takes people like you and me to believe that faith still works.

Chapter 1

Having a Relationship with God

David longed for God and His presence. David understood that the presence of God was worth more than anything in this life. David had everything as the king, but he knew the King of all kings. David the king said he would rather be a doorkeeper in the house of God, just to be in His presence. Titles will not mean a thing if you don't have a relationship with God.

Bradley and I both grew up as Anglicans, where we faithfully served in the church. Bradley was from Green Turtle Cay, and I was from Fox Town. At that time, there was a new priest who came to visit the church, and Bradley came along with him. We met in Fox Town when the priest came to the church there and afterwards, my mom prepared a meal to feed them. My mom just had a new baby, so being the oldest girl, I had to cook for them.

We both worked in the church from our younger days. I cleaned the church and made sure every Sunday morning the altar was decorated with fresh flowers. I helped with Sunday School and Youth Meeting. Bradley served as an altar boy. Although we worked in the church, we didn't understand anything about having a relationship with God.

As a young girl growing up, my parents had 14 children. I was the second child and the first girl, so I had to help with household chores and with taking care of my younger siblings. This was not easy and sometimes it was depressing. I didn't have any play time because there was always work to do. During those times, I was seeking the face of God. I told Him I didn't know how to serve Him but if He would teach me how, I would serve Him. God is willing to do anything we ask Him. All we have to do is believe. He will allow you to go through difficult times, not to destroy you, but to build your faith.

Chapter 2

They Thought I was Dead

I thank God for my parents who were both Christians and loved God. They instilled in me how to trust God in my life whenever there was trouble. My mom would always say, “Pray about it.” When I was a young girl, my mom told me I was in a coma. She told me I didn’t have any breath or pulse, and the doctors had already given up on me. The nurse was called in to confirm whether I was dead or not. When she came to check on me, she told them I had a slow heartbeat.

I was flown to Nassau to the hospital. Upon arriving at the hospital, I was checked in and placed in a small room. My mom overheard the doctors saying that they would leave me there until my heart stopped beating. She started crying because she thought I was gone.

Through all her tears, she remembered who God was and began to pray.

Shortly afterwards, the doctors came back to check on me. I was almost on the floor because I started to move, so they had to relocate me from the small room and place me in the ward. I still was unresponsive but had started to improve after a few days. I was able to hear, but I could not respond. I was being asked many questions, but I could not answer them. When I was able to open my eyes, it felt like I was sleeping. When I woke up, the doctors were in shock. The faith my parents had in God brought me back to life, and I am still alive today. They thought I was dead, but God was not finished with me. He had not started yet, and He had a plan for my life.

Chapter 3

Believing God for a Family

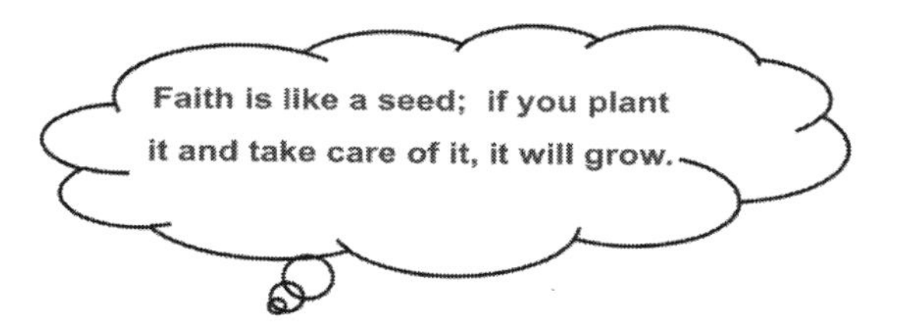

As a young girl, the Lord spoke to me, just like Samuel. I didn't know anything about God speaking to people. I would tell myself that it was all in my mind. There were times when the voice was so loud, I looked around to see who was there. When I met my husband, we both were very young, but I remembered the Lord speaking to me telling me that Bradley was going to be my husband. Just like Sarah, I laughed. After meeting him, he moved to another island. I started hearing from other people that he had other girlfriends, not just one, but many. I said to myself, "That was not God but my mind." Bradley and I remained friends and kept in close contact.

Bradley and I got married on August 7, 1976, and 47 years later, we are still together. After we got married, we moved to Marsh Harbour. We started visiting the Assembly of God Church there on Sunday nights. It was there that we learned about the Holy Spirit. I remember there was a guest preacher that first night, and the presence of God was in the church. People were just weeping while I was fighting not to cry. I didn't want my makeup to ruin and look messy. I heard someone call my name out loud. I looked around to see who called my name so loud in church. Nobody was paying attention to me, but when I heard it again, the voice said, "Look at you, allowing your makeup to come between us." I opened my heart and gave in to the Lord.

After that night, I never went to church with makeup on. When I share this story, I make sure to let people know that there is nothing wrong with wearing makeup, but please don't let anyone or anything come between you and your God. The only thing that matters is your relationship.

We had our first child, Cornelia, on August 5, 1977. After having our first child, we decided a few years later that we would have another child. The doctor told me I couldn't have any more children, especially since they could not figure out how I had the first one. The doctor said, "You will not have any more children." I acknowledged what he said and I went to God, asking Him for a son for my husband. A few months later, I went back to that doctor and told him I was pregnant. He laughed at me and told me that it was all in my head. After he examined me, he was very puzzled. He asked, "How did this happen? No one knew it at that time, but I was not only pregnant with one baby but two boys. The doctor didn't believe I was pregnant and didn't conduct a pelvic scan to confirm the results. At the time, I didn't believe in witchcraft, and I didn't engage anyone on my behalf. My parents taught me to trust God, and that is what I did.

I had to travel to Nassau to have the baby because we didn't have the faculty in Abaco at the time. I was living with my aunt while in Nassau, and I remembered her telling me, "You don't believe in witchcraft, but someone is trying to take you out." When she said that, I remembered the Lord allowed me to hear the lady telling someone she was going to "fix" me, but I didn't pay attention to it. I had a disgruntled customer who didn't like the price I charged her for some skirts. She was angry with me, saying that I charged her too much. She knew the cost before I made them. I told my aunt that no one could fix me; God would take care of me. I went into labor, and I was having no real pain except a little nagging pain in my back. I thank God for my aunt who took me to the hospital because she felt like something wasn't right when they examined me. The doctors were confused because I should have had more contractions, but shortly after I had the first baby. They still didn't know that there was another baby. One of my babies died because the doctor did not believe I was pregnant or that I was having twins. I was due in December, but my babies came in October, two months early. One of the babies died because he was left in too long. We named him Cornelius Anwar Reckley. I remember when they put me in the room, the young lady who was there said, “You know you have another baby in there.” God still works miracles because if I didn't trust God, my baby and I would have died.

Chapter 4

Cornelius Experienced the Hand of God

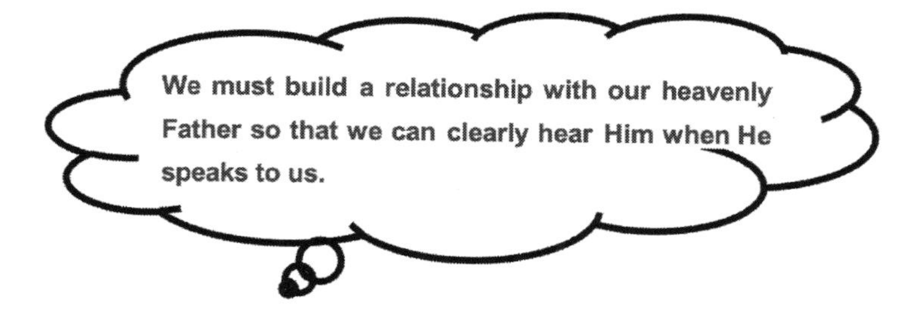

Whom God keeps is well kept, and today my son is 41 years old. After he was born, the enemy was still fighting for his life. He was born premature, and his ears were not developed properly. I had many challenges having to go to the doctor every few weeks. Finally, they decided that he needed surgery to correct the problem because it had affected his tonsils. My faith was being stretched again.

After he had the surgery, the doctor told me my son would be off balance for about six weeks. The next day, the doctor came to check up on him. They had to go look for him because he was on another ward watching TV. The doctor fussed him and told him he was supposed to be dizzy. The doctor asked him if his head was spinning. My son replied, "No." Cornelius told the doctor, "I know you put a tube in my throat." The doctor was shocked, wondering how he knew that because he should have been asleep. He said, "I watched you put the tube in." The doctor couldn't figure out how he knew about the tube. The surgery was supposed to last about one and a half hours. However, they operated on him for almost six hours. The doctor said if he didn't come when he did he would have trouble for the rest of his life. They told me he would not be able to shower or go swimming because he couldn't let water get in his ear. My son had a speedy recovery. God is truly faithful, and today He can do all those things that they said He couldn't do. As a result of this situation, my faith grew.

The enemy continued to fight for the life of my son. A few years ago, I was at work, but I was talking to the Lord and I heard Him say to me, "The enemy is about to attack." He didn't say anything else to me. I told my children not to call me in the morning at work because I was busy. However, this morning, the phone rang and

I said to the staff member who answered, "That's my son." She asked, "How did you know?" I asked her to give me the phone as she was telling him to hang up the phone. I took the phone from her and as soon as he started to talk, I knew something was wrong. I asked him what happened, and he said, "Mom, please come." I don't know how I got home so fast. I will never forget that day. When I arrived home, he was standing in the doorway, unable to move. He looked like someone threw a bucket of water over him. His collarbone area looked like someone was inside his body pulling in from the inside out. My son is big in stature, but somehow I was able to lift him and put him in the vehicle and take him to the clinic. This was his first attack of asthma. If the Holy Spirit didn't speak to me that morning, he was going to die because he could not breathe. While on the way to the clinic, I prayed and asked the Lord to heal my son. This was his first and last asthma attack. I thank God for His healing.

Chapter 5

My First Restaurant and God's Favor

When I had my first restaurant in 1982, someone wanted to buy shares in the business, which appeared to be a good idea. The day they brought the check, I prayed and told God what I wanted; I didn't consult with Him. I told Him, “If this is not what I should do, please show me a sign.” I finished making up my deposit and left to go to the bank. One of the staff members called me, saying I left the check and the cash in the book. I completed running my errands for the day, then went back to the shop. I was startled that the check was gone. I never found that check again. Be encouraged. God is well able to do all He promised to do. I called the lady and told her I had to cancel the arrangements.

Sometimes, because our backs are against the wall,

we will make a permanent decision in a temporary moment. We must take the time to go to God first. God will always make ways for you when you're faithful. David said, "When you delight yourself in the Lord, He will give you the desires of your heart." He will direct your path and give you the tools that you need.

I experienced this when I started my first restaurant. I was working at Standard Hardware at the time and when I got off from work, I would make pizza. It grew so fast that it was hard to keep up with it. The people loved the pizza because it was different. One day while at work, a lady came looking for me and said, "I heard you need a place to open your pizza business." I thought to myself, "I didn't say anything to anyone about opening a business." That woman was not a Christian, but God used her to get me where He wanted me to be. She said, "I have a building, but I would have to fix it up. We will not charge you rent until you open the business." I was shocked because I didn't have a conversation with her. I thought to myself, "I have the location but I don't have the money."

I went to the bank with no collateral. All I had was my faith in God. I had a meeting with the bank manager and told him my plan. I walked out of that bank with the money that I needed. He told me he wanted to hire me to work in the bank because of my personality. I told him I had to bring my dreams to reality. God is faithful! People came from all over the island to enjoy the food from Lovely's Pizza. The favor of God is more than money; it will open doors. This was a ministry for me as well as a business. It was at this place that I started the Feed the Children Program. I hired single moms and young people who were trying to go away to school. I hired them to help them, and sometimes I didn't get a paycheck. God is faithful!

You can have all the riches this world can offer, but if you don't have Jesus, you are poor. We will die and leave it all behind. People are so greedy as they plot and plan for this life. If it looks like you have more than they have, they will watch your business. If it looks like it's growing and prospering, they will try all they can to destroy you and your business.

Chapter 6

Personal Testimony of Healing from Migraines and Bursitis

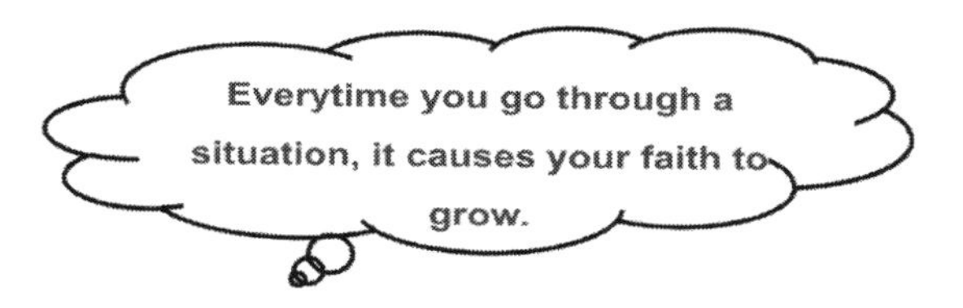

For many years I suffered from migraine headaches that were so intense and lasted for many days. My doctor sent me away to get a CAT scan done. Upon returning home with the lab results to take back to the doctor, the nurse looked at the results and almost fell out. She asked me, "Did you take a flight to get back home?" She said I shouldn't have been allowed to fly. She showed me the X-ray results, explaining that all the white spots that were showing were my blood vessels that were swollen. She told me I had to go home and go to bed and not do anything.

It was impossible for me to follow her command because I was a wife and a mother. One Sunday I went to church and was not feeling well because I was having one of those terrible headaches. In fact, I was not going to church, but the Lord told me to get up and go. I followed His instructions that Sunday morning, and I was delivered from migraines. My head was hurting so bad it felt like someone was squeezing my brain. I heard the voice of the Lord say, "Get up and go to the restroom." I got up and went to the restroom. When I got inside, I went to the toilet and felt like something broke loose within me. I left that headache in that restroom and never had another one.

I remember I was diagnosed with bursitis, which was a very painful experience. When it flared up, it felt like someone was in my joints with a fire. The pain was in all my joints, then it went up in my neck and then to my spine. I started wearing a very soft neck brace at first. Then every few months, I had to change it until it got to the very hard one. It was uncomfortable, and I suffered from this pain for years. It got so bad that I couldn't lift my hands.

The doctor wanted to do surgery on my spine because the bones were rubbing together. They told me it was a fifty-fifty chance I could be crippled for the rest of my life. I told them, "I am going to put my trust in God." As a final recourse, the doctors sent me to a specialist who dealt with arthritis. They wanted me to try some new medication that just came out. They were unsure of what the side effects were going to be. That day I said to God, "I know that You didn't create me to live like this. I need You to heal me." I couldn't comb my daughter's hair when the pain got so bad. The doctor gave me shots in my joints to help. I remember the last shot I took in my neck, and the next day I couldn't turn my head because I was having spasms. It was crazy, and I cried out to God, and He heard my prayers. I couldn't lift my hands to praise God for months. One Sunday, I went to church, and during the praise and worship time, I don't remember putting my hands up, but when I caught myself, my hands were in the air. I began to give God glory and praise. I was delivered that day from that disease.

Chapter 7

Surgery for Fibroids and Healing from Appendicitis

One of the things that caused my faith to really grow was a surgery I had in 1991. I was having serious pain in my back and stomach. My monthly cycle was very painful, which came three to six times per month. When I was younger, I did not have a period. This was the reason why the doctor said that I could not have children. I went to the doctor but they couldn't find anything wrong. However, this situation kept getting worse. I went from not seeing a period for months at a time—and when it did come, it would last about two days with hardly any bleeding— to something totally different. Now my period would last for days, and the bleeding was so bad I was afraid to travel. Finally, I decided to go to Nassau to see a doctor. As soon as she touched my stomach, she found out what the problem was. I had fibroids. She told me she felt a few of them, but one was in the cancerous stage, and I needed to have an emergency surgery. She was upset that the doctor that I was previously attending could not tell me that I had to get a scan done. The technician who was conducting the pelvic scan said to me, "Ma'am I'm not supposed to tell you but, if you already have children, I would recommend that you get a hysterectomy." She told me that I had so many fibroids that I had a tree of little ones growing. If I had allowed them just to remove the fibroids in short order, they would have to cut me again. In all things, God can be glorified. It was because of this surgery I truly understood what faith in God was all about.

While in the hospital, there was a group of women who came to the hospital and prayed with patients before they went into surgery. One of those women came to pray with me. She could sense that I was afraid. She said to me, "Do you know that if you ask God to come and hold your hand, He will come and He will take away your fear?" I prayed, and in seconds, my fears were gone. I had surgery on Thursday, and a lady who was visiting her family asked me when I was going to have surgery. I told her I already did. She didn't believe me and said, "No, you didn't have surgery." The nurse who was nearby replied, "Yes, she had surgery already but she doesn't look like it." My doctor had to go away on Friday, but she came early Saturday morning to check me out. When she looked at the cut she said, "Oh my God." I thought something was wrong because she kept saying that. I asked her what was wrong. She said, "Nothing is wrong. The cut has already healed." She couldn't figure out how the cut healed so fast since I was supposed to be in the hospital for a week. I was discharged that Sunday, and she said what was happening had nothing to do with her.

About two weeks after the surgery, I returned home and started having serious pain in my stomach. I went to the doctor and found out that my appendix was infected. I was told that I had to go and get it taken out. I told the devil, "I am not going back under the knife. I will not do another surgery again. I will trust the Lord." The devil doesn't like it when you take a stand to trust God. I didn't go back to the doctor. I told the devil, "I didn't ask for it, so I am not signing for it. Take it back to the pit." And that was the end of that. Several years later, I started having serious pain again and a fever. I went to the doctor, who told me that I needed to get to Nassau. I needed surgery for the same thing I prayed for. I went to Nassau to the hospital, and while I was waiting, I said to my Father God, I told the devil, "I am not having any more surgeries. I am putting my trust in God." They had me hooked up to drip and were ready to admit me to the ward, but they had one more test to do. While they were conducting the scan, I heard the technician say, "I don't see anything here." My appendix is still where it was originally. God is really faithful.

Miracles should be the norm of our life. We should be concerned when we don't see or experience them. When sickness or disease comes upon us, our first thing should be to go to God. According to His Word, when Jesus died, He carried our sickness and disease. The Word declares that by His stripes we are healed, so we have to believe that and live like we believe it.

Chapter 8

A Miraculous Healing from a Broken Collarbone

When you go to the gym, you start working out with the light weights, and then you increase the weight. Faith is just like that.

Cornelia June, my oldest daughter, was always a strong-willed child. I was in labor for one week with her. She was born at home on the island of Abaco. I remembered the night my father-in-law told the doctor. "If she doesn't have the baby tonight, I am taking her into Nassau." I didn't want to go to Nassau, so I prayed and asked God to please help me that night. Cornelia was born that very night, which was a very fast delivery. She made sure everyone heard her, letting them know she had arrived. The doctor held her up by her two little feet, and she urinated right on him. He couldn't stop laughing while he looked at her and said, "She is the first baby that I don't have to bathe." She was so clean from head to toe. She was the first girl that was born into my husband's family.

There was always something going on with Cornelia. She always did the opposite of what she was told to do. She was a free-spirited child, who kept us on our toes. She worked with me in our restaurant. One day I allowed her to take the day off to play in a softball game. She was supposed to come back for the evening shift, but she didn't want to come to work in the restaurant, so Bradley went to get her. She told him she quit, and he told her, she better get to work. They got into an argument, and he took his belt off to punish her. He believed in using the rod for discipline. She was embarrassed because all of her friends were there, so she decided to fight the beating. Somehow, she fell down and her collarbone was broken.

The doctor sent us to Nassau, saying she needed surgery to put pins to hold the bones together. That's what the doctor said, but let me tell you, on that flight going into Nassau, I began talking to the Lord. I told Him two things: "I don't have the time nor the money for surgery." I also asked Him to please let the bones be back together on the X-ray. When we got to the hospital and the doctor read the letter, he looked at the X-ray, and then at the letter again. He asked, "What foolish doctor sent you to the hospital?" He showed us the X-ray, which was normal. The doctor at home showed us the X-ray with the bone broken into two parts. One part was hanging, and the other part was sticking up. The X-ray the doctor showed us in Nassau showed the bones were back together.

God is so good! We returned home the next day while the doctor was off the island. He called me and said that he heard that we were back home. I told him I believed in God, and that I got a miracle. His response was, "I don't care who you believe in, get her back to Nassau because she needs to have that surgery." So I told him, "I will take her back where we did the first X-ray." I wanted them to take another X-ray, but when I got there, the young lady who did the first X-ray asked if we were still on the island because her collarbone was broken. I told her what happened, and she did another X-ray. She came back with the results and said, "This is the first miracle I have ever seen where the bones were back together."

Chapter 9

Teenage Pregnancy and Forgiveness

As believers, the enemy is after us, and if he can't get us, he will go after our seed. When Corneila was 18 and just finished high school, we wanted her to go to college. She couldn't go anymore because she got pregnant. I remember one night I heard someone call my name. I thought it was my husband, but when I checked, he was sleeping. I laid down to go back to sleep, and I heard the voice call me again. He said, "I stopped by to let you know that your daughter is pregnant." He called her by name and I got angry. In my heart, I had already planned to tell her she had to leave our home because she knew better. He said, "You show her love. She did the act but I gave life." I reminded Him about the times that I prayed and asked Him to keep her. He responded to me by saying,

"I have everything in control." I asked, "How could everything be in control? When her daddy finds out, he is going to kill her." He told me again, "Everything is under control."

I couldn't sleep anymore, so I got up early, and as soon as she was up, I told her she was pregnant. That didn't go well because she told me that's all I was thinking about. She said, "I just saw my period, so I know I am not pregnant." This tension and disagreement continued for about two months. I noticed that she continued to buy pads, so I said to God, "You told me she is pregnant, but she is still buying pads." He told me to watch the box. I asked, "Why do I have to watch the box?" She was not using them.

One day I heard the voice of God telling me, "She is going to Nassau to have an abortion. Don't let her do it." He told me to call my sister. I was told which sister to call and I did that. I called her and told her my daughter was coming to town and why she was coming. She didn't believe me. My daughter went into Nassau, got on the bus with her uncle, and they went looking for an abortion clinic. They saw the clinic and then got off the bus, but they could not find the clinic.

Corneila told me afterwards that she was so afraid of a confrontation with her dad, so she thought that was the best thing to do. Cornelia and her uncle ended up going to the same sister that I was led by the Lord to call. She told her, "Your mommy knows that you're pregnant." She asked me what I wanted her to do. I told her to come home. God always has everything in place, no matter how it looks.

This was really a dark time for me while the church folks talked so badly about me instead of praying for me. I remember not wanting to go out to church anywhere. The voice of God spoke to me, and said, "Hold your head up. You are a living example to her, and you taught her the right way. Don't let anyone make you feel like you did something wrong." The enemy was trying to destroy my daughter's life. He couldn't get to me, so he decided that he was going to work through her. Parents, remember when you walk with the Lord, you have an enemy that's real. Your husband or your children are not your enemies. He wants your children. My daughter and I didn't have a good relationship, but I didn't give up. I kept trusting God.

Chapter 10

God's Provision for Baby Shawnelia

After Corneila had her first child, she was still single but decided to move out of our home, and she took her baby with her. The baby was always sickly, so one day the Lord told me to take the baby and raise her and teach her about Him. I told the Lord, "She's a baby." I said to Him, "I didn't want any more babies crying around my head." He told me again, "I want you to take care of her, and I will take care of you." Christmas was coming and I had set aside a few dresses for which I was paying on. I had 50 dollars and the Lord spoke to me and told me to go get the dresses. Someone had already brought a few dresses for Shawnelia, so I was not going to need the ones on layaway for a while. He insisted that I go now. I turned the car around and went into the store, I paid for the dresses and was left with two dollars. As I was walking out of the store, the Lord told me to look down. When I did, I saw a fifty-dollar bill in front of me. He said, "I want you to see that I can take care of her and I will take care of you." To many people, 50 dollars might not look like much, but to me, that meant so much.

I want you to know that God hears everything and He remembers. Growing up as a young girl, I said to the Lord, "If I ever get married, please don't give me a lot of children." I had four children, and my youngest baby was maturing where she could take care of herself. Now the Lord was telling me to take a baby. I said, "Lord, Cornelia needs to take care of her own baby." Trying to reason with Him, I said, "Lord, you know my husband said that he is not taking the baby. So if you want me to take the baby, you will have to speak to him." A few days later, my husband came and said to me, "Go get the baby and bring her home." I know that God has a plan for her life, and the devil was trying to destroy her before she was born. Shawnelia had many challenges. At about nine months, she had salmonella, which kills adults, but she survived it as a baby. It was so amazing how the Lord worked it out.

I had a lump in my breast and the doctors were treating it as a cyst, but they soon realized that it was something more serious. I had to travel to Nassau to the hospital, so I decided to take Shawnelia with me. My husband told me to leave her because I was going to the doctor. At that time she had a fever. I was convinced that the fever would leave and she would be okay. Again I heard the voice of God telling me to take her with me. I told my husband, "I will take her with me." After we got into Nassau, the fever came back. The next day I left Shawnelia with a babysitter while I went to a doctor's appointment. I checked with the babysitter, and I was told that the baby was doing fine.

After I was finished with the doctor, we picked up the baby and she still had the fever. She was passing stuff that had blood in it, and I didn't know what to do. I went to the bathroom and prayed. I said to the Lord, "If I need to take her to the hospital, please speak to my sister when I come out of the bathroom." My sister said, "We need to take her to the hospital." When she got there and the medical team saw what was coming out of the baby, they called in a specialist. They ran numerous tests on her all night until about five o'clock in the morning. At that time they were able to tell me the results of the tests. I can tell you, God worked that out because if she had been home by the time they found out what was wrong with her, she would have probably died. The doctor told me I needed surgery for the lump in my breast, but I had to deal with my granddaughter first to make sure she was okay. God healed her little body. When I came back home, I told God I didn't have the money for the surgery. In fact, I reminded Him I told the devil I was not going back under the knife. I got up the next morning, realizing that the lump was gone.

After a while, I checked my breast again and I found two other lumps. I started seeing the doctor, and they were monitoring one of the lumps that was growing rapidly. I was really getting depressed just going through with the first lump God healed me from. A few weeks earlier, I was right back there again. After a few visits, I said to the devil, "Back up. We already went down this road before, and I am not going back there with this." I stopped going to the doctor and decided to trust God. Those lumps went back just where they came from. I gave my God all the glory.

CHAPTER 11

FAITH FOR MY MARRIAGE

Life was not easy for me, but I loved God enough to trust the process. My husband and I have been married for 47 years, and it was not always easy. There were many thorns along the way. We didn't have any major problems until the middle of our marriage. It was like hell was unleashed in our home. There was no peace, and we were constantly fussing about everything. We were both Christians, but we had allowed our hearts to be angry and bitter towards one another. That was food for the enemy to work with, and we gave him plenty of ammunition to fight with. Things got so bad that I told my husband I was leaving because I was tired of fighting and tired of the confusion. Sometimes we were trying to figure out what we were fighting over. The enemy is after marriages and we can't give in to him. We had to fight for our marriage as Christians. We have to understand that Satan is after both of us, and he will use us to destroy each other if we allow him.

I remember one day talking to Abba about our situation and He said to me, "Your husband is not your enemy. The enemy is using you both to destroy one another." From that day, I started to look at things differently. I was going to leave and not look back. So many people walk out on their marriage when they should be fighting for their marriage. We have to fight to keep ourselves as Christians, and it's the same with our marriage. In the same way that we have faith in God for everything else, we need to have faith to keep our marriage as Christians. When we live according to the Word of God, the enemy will not have a thing to fight us with as long as we submit one to another. As Scripture instructs, we should *submit ourselves "one to another in the fear of God. Wives, submit yourself unto your own husband, as unto the Lord.... Husbands, love your wives, even as Christ also loved the church and gave himself for it" (Ephesians 5: 21-22, 25).*

Our marriage is very important to the enemy. We must recognize that he will not go after unbelievers because he already has them. It's the believer's marriage he is after. My husband and I both knew we didn't want to end in divorce, so we submitted our marriage to God and asked Him to help us. Our marriage is cemented in our faith. In Him, we know that He can keep us. I thank God for my husband. He is a man who truly loves God and seeks to serve Him. He is dedicated to doing kingdom business. When we love and serve God, the enemy is always trying to trip us up.

Chapter 12

Cornelia's Cancer Story

He is the God of restoration. My daughter got married and moved to another island. She called me crying one day, saying that her husband wanted a baby girl. The doctor wanted to freeze her uterus because she had active cancer cells. I prayed and decided to believe in God. They sent us to a specialist who worked with cancer. When he examined her, he said he could see the scars, but the cancer was gone. I told her, "It's up to you whether you want to believe the doctor's report, or you can trust God. You can have your baby girl after that conversation." A month later, she called me saying, "Mom, I am pregnant." Don't tell me that God is not real and that He doesn't speak to His people. He is real!

After she had her baby girl, whose name was

Lannekka, she was diagnosed with stage four cancer a few years later. The nurse told her, "You are too far gone, and your mommy can't pray this one off you." I told her to tell that nurse, "The God that I serve raised the dead, so this is a small thing for Him to do." Cornelia had to go to Nassau to see the specialist. He did the biopsy and sent it away. He told her it would be two weeks for the report to find out what type of cancer it was. He told her they would send the report to her doctor. A week later, she received a phone call from the doctor. He said, "I had to call you because the results are in and not a trace of cancer was found." God is so real, and there's none like Him.

Chapter 13

God's Favor on Shawnelia

My granddaughter is now a mother of two children. The enemy tried to take her out with both of her babies. After she had her first child, a baby boy, Shario Bradley Albury, she went to use the bathroom and they found her unconscious and bleeding on the floor. It was later discovered that a piece of the afterbirth was left inside her. While having her second child, she was in labor, experiencing very intense pain for about two days. I prayed and asked God to please send the doctor because I knew something was wrong. She asked the nurse to call the doctor but the nurse told her she didn't need the doctor. Shortly after that, the doctor was passing and she called out to him. He came to her and she told him that she was having pain. He asked her, "How long were you in labor?" She replied and he rushed her to surgery for an emergency C-section. They found the umbilical cord was wrapped around the baby's neck twice and couldn't move. The baby was safely delivered after the cord was unwrapped from around the neck. Shawnelia had a baby girl and named her Voneya Sabrea Lovely Bain.

God is so amazing. I started a restaurant in 2013 to help with the Feed the Children Program. It grew so rapidly because the people loved the food. In 2018, I wanted to retire from the restaurant. I was still doing the Feed the Children Program at that time. I thought my daughter would have taken it on, but she didn't want it, so I was going to close it. My granddaughter told me she would take it over. I was so shocked because she was young and didn't like the kitchen. She took it on, learned to cook, and ran that business like a professional. She truly is a great mother to her children. She always puts them first.

Chapter 14

Healing from Colon Cancer

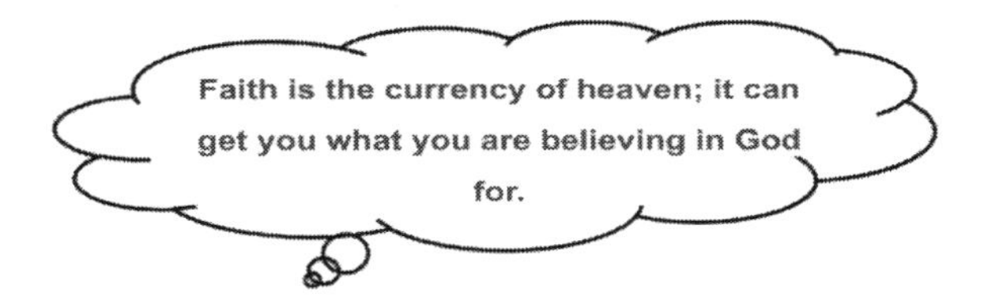

In 2003, I was diagnosed with colon cancer. A few years before that, I was talking to the Lord and He said, "The enemy is going to attack you with cancer." At that time, there was hardly anything spoken about cancer. So I asked, "What am I supposed to do?" He said, "Trust Me."

A few years passed and I had forgotten about it. I started having serious pain, and I didn't go to the doctor right away. I waited until it was really unbearable. The doctor treated me for a while, giving me some heavy painkillers. The pills were not doing much for me, and then finally the doctor told me that I had colon cancer. I had to do some testing and also needed a colonoscopy. I went to the doctor in Nassau and they told me that something was there. They had to do the test to find what stage and what type of cancer it was.

I went to service on a Sunday morning, at Bahamas Faith Ministries, where Dr. Myles Munroe was the pastor. As I sat there in the service, I was talking to God. I asked Him to please let Dr. Munroe call a prayer line for healing after he was finished preaching. Dr. Munroe gave an altar call, and he was closing out the service while the praise team was singing. He told them to stop and said, "I have to obey the Father because there is someone that needs to be delivered from their infirmity." He called for the person to come. Other people came and he prayed for everyone, but he came back to me and told me three times, "Your father wants you to know that you're delivered from your infirmity this day." I had to do a colonoscopy the following Monday morning. They put me to sleep at about nine o'clock, and I woke up at about noon. The technician who was conducting the test called another person to look at the results. He said he had never seen a colon so clean, not even a baby. God had stepped in and healed my colon. They were so shocked that they refused to take the balance of the funds that I owed them for the procedure. God is still working miracles. We must have faith in God. There are people who try to make you believe that God stopped performing miracles. The Bible says that He is the same today as He was yesterday. He doesn't change.

As Jesus said,

> "Therefore I say unto you, What things soever ye desire, when ye pray, believe that you receive them, and ye shall have them. And when you stand praying, forgive if ye have ought against any: that your Father also which is in heaven may forgive you your trespasses. But if ye don't forgive, neither will your Father which is in heaven forgive your trespasses" (Mark 11:24-26).

We have to believe that God is who He says that He is, and He wants to heal us. In 3 John 1: 2, it says, "Beloved, I wish above all things that thou mayest prosper and be in good health even as thy soul prospereth."

We don't have to take the doctor's report. We can believe the report of the Lord. His report says that by the stripes of Jesus, we are healed. As Isaiah 53:5 says, "But he was wounded for our transgressions, he was bruised for our iniquities, the chastisement of our peace was upon him and by his stripes we are healed."

Chapter 15

Chandel, My Gift from God

My youngest daughter, Chandel Isabel, was a gift from God. I remember when the doctor told me I was pregnant with her; I cried. I was recovering from a horrible pregnancy, and my baby was only one year and three months old. I said to God, "I only asked for one son, and I don't want another baby." I had a good pregnancy, and after she was born, she was the best baby I had ever seen. She was not fussy and allowed me to do what I needed to do. She hardly ever cried.

When she was about six years old, we had to move her from the school that she was attending because the teacher was giving her a hard time. We couldn't understand why because she was such a sweet child. We couldn't help but love her. We enrolled her in the government school where she adjusted very well. One day she came home from school and said to me, “There are children coming to school without lunch.” I didn't pay any attention to her. I had a restaurant, and I catered to the school every day. She came home and would talk about these children often. So one day I decided to deliver the lunch as usual and took a few extra ones with me. When I got to school, I saw a lot of children just standing around. It was lunchtime, but they had no lunch. So I asked why they didn't have lunch, and I was told they didn't have any money to buy lunch. From that day on, I made up my mind that no child would go hungry. I had to stop selling lunch so that I could prepare lunch for those children who couldn’t afford it. I found out between the two schools that there were about 70 children. If we did not move our Chandell, I wouldn't have known that there were children who were going hungry.

She had a smile that would light up any room. I remember one day the Lord told me to tell her that He gave everyone a gift, and her gift was her smile. Everyone remembered her smile. About two weeks before she passed, the Lord told me to tell her He loved her so much. He placed her in time for eternity. That was a wake-up call for me, and a reminder that we all will pass through time for eternity. We all have to be ready.

In December 2005, two days before Christmas, this sweet little girl was snatched away from us. It was the hardest thing in my life to know that my baby was gone and there was nothing that I could do to bring her back. My husband and I had just left to go away for our vacation. We were driving into Mississippi to see some friends, and we had only gotten as far as Orlando. While we were shopping for a few things for our trip, Bradley asked me to get Chandell a few things, but every time I would pick up the items for her, I kept hearing "wait" in my spirit. I decided that I would wait until we were passing back this way. I told my husband I couldn't stop thinking about "Channie." That was her nickname. It felt like she was there with us while driving.

I picked up my phone, and I noticed that I had a voice message from my oldest daughter. She wanted me to call her. I thought it was her and her husband having a problem. The voice of the Lord said to me, "It's Channie. She is gone." I thought He meant that she left the island and went to Nassau. He said, "No, she is in eternity." My heart dropped. I tried calling everyone that I could think of to call, but I didn't get any answer. Finally, my son called, and I told him she was gone. I just needed to know what had happened. They were confused and wanted to know how I knew. God is so real to me, and He gave us a peace that we could not explain. He wrapped His arms of love around us and never let us go. We truly miss her, but we know that God did all things well. I told Him, "Thanks for loaning her to me." I was so grateful that He allowed me to be her mom.

After she passed, the following year on Mother's Day, I got up and looked across from my kitchen window and saw the most beautiful lilies I had ever seen. My daughter knew that I loved them. In fact, I had a beautiful garden, but I didn't have lilies in it. I was so grateful to see them. The following year, the same thing happened, and I could not explain where they came from. Life was not easy, but I had to learn to live one day at a time.

Chapter 16

Healing in My Spine and Face

After the death of my daughter, I really was missing her. It became even harder the next year when I was diagnosed with breast cancer. It was crazy. After being diagnosed, I decided that I was just going to trust God. It was not easy and very painful. I remembered the word from the Lord during that time. It seemed like everything that could go wrong was going wrong. I went to see a doctor who practiced natural medicine. He conducted a full body scan. When the results came back, he asked if I walked into his office. He said there was no way I was supposed to be walking with my spine being out of alignment. It was painful to walk but I kept going.

The doctors recommended that I stay in the USA for one week to take a test every four hours because my health was so bad. I told them, "I am going home. I will take my chances with God." Can I tell you, I went home that day, and I will never forget it. On July fourth, Change Ministry was having a women's conference, and the Lord told me to go out that night. I didn't want to go because I was in so much pain. I went to the service, and I received my healing that night. I could not sit up in bed. In order for me to get out of bed, I had to roll out of bed. But that night when I got home and laid down, I was able to sit up. I was so excited. I told my husband, "Look, I can get up!" God is indeed faithful.

As soon as I was getting over one situation and I thought all was well, I had to face something else. One day I noticed I had a few black spots on my face. One of them was right next to my nose. I thought they were beauty spots, so I didn't pay them any attention for a while. Then out of the blue, the one that was close to my nose started to grow rapidly. It started to be painful, and then I noticed that two more started to grow. I went to the doctor, and as soon as he looked at it, he told me it was cancerous and I had to get them removed. I reminded the Lord that I told Satan that I was not going back under the knife. I told the Lord He had to do it again. I will never forget it. One day I was touching them, and they all dropped off my face in my hand. I didn't have to go back to the doctor.

We serve a God who is real. He told us to remind Him of His Word. It is not that He forgets, but that He wants us to know His Word. He said that He watches over His Word to perform it. Get to know the Word of God. No matter what you are going through, you can find help and hope in the Word of God.

Chapter 17

Miracles in China While Sharing the Gospel

One of the things I enjoy doing in my free time is reading. I remember reading a book about China and its culture. I read about how the women would bind their feet because they thought it was beautiful and sexy. This was not sexy but sad because so many of them became crippled. I said I would love to go to China as a missionary. In 2008, the Lord granted me the opportunity to go to China. Bahamas Agriculture and Industrial Corporation (commonly known as BAIC) offered me the opportunity to take up a training course in craft and machine embroidery for three months. The favor of God is more than money. I received an all-expenses paid trip to China. There were people from 50 different nations and I was there with them.

I had the opportunity to share the Word of God in Bible Study and Sunday morning service in communist China, which was an awesome experience. There were people from many different religions, and I was able to share the gospel and help them understand who my God is. I remember the first day I arrived in China. I was at the front desk to check something out. I met one of the ladies from Africa at the desk. She was trying to get the front desk clerks to understand that she needed some medicine. The people at the desk could not understand her. While I was standing there, the voice of God spoke to me to tell her, "If she believes, she will not need that medicine anymore." I felt like I couldn't tell her that because I didn't know her. He told me again to tell her, so I went to her and told her what He said. She looked at me and said, "Thank you" and left.

Early the next morning, I heard someone knocking on my door. It was the same lady I spoke with the day before. She told me after she left and went to her room, she felt something like fire going through her body. She received her healing and didn't need the medicine anymore. She told me about her husband who was sick for six years. She couldn't tell her family about him being sick because they would have made her leave him. She said for six years he couldn't have sex with her, but she remained faithful to him. I told her that while we were there, we would fast one day out of the week for his healing. She got the call two weeks before we left saying that he went to the doctor, and they could not find a trace of the sickness in his body. God is real!

While in China, I shared the gospel with some Rastafarians who gave their hearts to the Lord. There was a young lady who was from one of the Caribbean islands. She testified that when she came to China she attended church but didn't have a relationship with God. She was so happy with the teaching I shared that changed her life. I was so grateful to God for the opportunity to make a difference in the lives of the people I met there.

There was a young lady from Palestine. She said in her country, people were either a Muslim or a Christian. She said that they carried the name of Christian but didn't practice it. When I first met her, she was very rude and was always trying to upset me. One day she was very rude, and I was going to let her have it. The Spirit told me to zip my lip. I didn't want to be obedient that day but I walked away and left her. Another day I was sitting on the patio, studying my Bible, and I felt these arms come around me. She said, "I want you to know that you are so different." She told me the young people were talking about me and wanted to be like me. I was so happy that I listened to the Lord. I was able to demonstrate the love of God, which was able to draw others to want to serve Him.

CHAPTER 18

MY MONEY MIRACLE

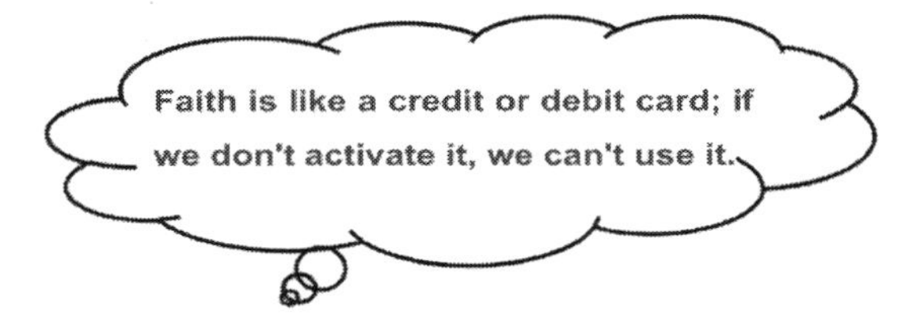

I don't care what you're going through; if you can activate your faith and pray, God will do it for you. Whatever your problem is, He can fix it. I remember I wasn't working, and I needed some money to pay some bills. I went to my heavenly Father and told Him I needed some money to pay bills. He said to me, "Go and put your hand in your jeans pocket." I told Him, "I don't have anything in my pocket." He told me again, "Go and put your hand in your pocket." I got up from lying on the bed and went to my jeans. I only had one pair of jeans, and when I pushed my hand in that pocket and pulled it out, there was a roll of US dollar bills. My first thought was why would my husband put his money in my pocket? I left that money there for one week. The Lord spoke to me and said, "The money is yours." I went back to the pocket and counted it out, which amounted to a few thousand dollars.

The Bible says that we have all been given the same measure of faith (see Romans 12:3). We have to learn to trust God when we can't trace Him. We must trust. Sometimes we are praying for things and it seems like our prayers are not being answered. We still have to believe that God will answer. When Daniel was praying to God, he prayed for 21 days. The angel came and told him that God answered from the first day he prayed. We have to remember that Satan is the prince of the air, who fights our prayers so that we will doubt God. Whatever you set before the throne of God, don't give up. Your answer is on the way. I want you to be encouraged because God is always with us. We just have to stay faithful.

Chapter 19

Faith and Obedience in Giving

I remember one day I was washing my dishes and talking to the Lord. He told me to go and take some corned beef to a particular lady. He called her name and I said, "I don't know where she lives." He said, "You know where she works." I told Him, "I will take her some money," but He insisted that I carry the corned beef. He told me to do it now. I got a box and started packing. He told me to put the corned beef on the top. I went to the place where she worked, but she was not at work. I said, "Okay, Lord, I have the stuff for her, but she is not here. Can I go back home now?" He told me to take them to her house. I drove into Murphy Town, and at the first house I saw, I stopped to ask if they knew where she lived. I was told she lived right in the house where I stopped. I got out of the car and walked to the house with the box of stuff. When she saw me and opened that box, the tears began to flow. She said, "I was here washing my dishes and telling the Lord if I only had some corned beef to cook." I had to join her in tears. God cares and He wanted to restore her faith. Shortly after that, she died. We need to not only have faith but be obedient in whatever He tells us to do. Just do it.

Chapter 20

Surviving Hurricane Dorian

On August 31, 2019, our lives changed forever. My husband suffered a stroke. Through it all, we saw the hand of God at work. The enemy meant it for bad, but God used it for our good. I was away for a few days when I noticed the tropical depression had turned into a hurricane. I called my husband and asked him if I should come home. I was due to return on that Saturday, but I felt like I should go home earlier. He told me it looked like the hurricane was coming to Abaco, so we should stay away until it passed. I felt so strongly that I needed to be home, so I prayed and asked God if I should go home to just speak to Bradley. He called me and told me to come home. I made plans for the next day and arrived home Friday evening. I could see my husband was not himself, but he said that he was tired.

We went to bed and he got up earlier than usual to pray. When I got up, he was coming into the bedroom and started to say something, but he couldn't get his words out. I realized he was having a stroke, so I rushed him to the doctor. We had to fly him out right away. Shortly after we left Abaco, the airport was closed. The sad part about this is he went in on an emergency flight on Saturday, but no doctor checked on my husband until that Tuesday. It appeared that they left him to die, but thank God for his mercy. Unfortunately, Bradley had another stroke while being overlooked in the hospital. The second stroke caused him to be paralyzed on his right side. The doctor told him that he would never walk again. I told the doctor they didn't know the God we served, who is more than able.

When the hurricane passed through Abaco, we lost our home and everything that we owned, along with our vehicle. It was a hard time for me while my husband was lying in the hospital. Our home was gone, and it was hopeless to look at. I can tell you, we never lost our faith in God. We remembered Job in the Bible who had lost everything but kept his faith in God. It was God who had blessed us, and it was Him who allowed it to be taken. So we knew we were in good hands. If my husband didn't have the stroke, we would have all died in our home during the storm. We were told that a tornado hit our home and took the roof off. We didn't find anything afterwards since we had about eight feet of water in the house. God is so amazing. He had it all worked out. When it didn't look good, He had everything under control.

My husband and I both had business in the same building, and God was so merciful that He spared the building. It had some damage that we were able to get repaired. We were able to turn his office into a bedroom, which gave us somewhere to lay our heads. Thank God for His blessings. We were off the island for three months while my husband had to attend therapy sessions. We spent one month in Nassau, and then we stayed with friends in the United States who took care of us for two months. Returning back home was not easy. There was so much to go through to get back to normal. It was hard to pick up the pieces that were badly damaged. I thank God for my church family who truly were a blessing to us. When we were about to return home after being gone for about three months, I told my pastor's wife I was coming home. She got some of the ladies together and got our room set up with a bed to sleep on. They always checked on us and now some of them are just like family.

So many homes were totally destroyed; so many lives were lost. It was the worst hurricane we ever experienced in the Bahamas, and so many people are still trying to get it together. There were so many donations, but so little got to the people who really needed it. I just want to encourage you to always keep your faith in God. He will never leave you. We all have our tests to go through. When someone is going through one, we should support them because your time is coming. God has proven Himself to us after the hurricane.

The pandemic came when so many people were just starting to get back on their feet. When everything was shut down, we truly had to depend on our relationship with God to be able to stand. After the hurricane, so many people were dying from stress because it was too much to handle. My husband had to shut his business down because he could no longer work. When we came home, we were trying to register with the Red Cross, but we were told that they could not do it. There were places for all the illegals to be registered, but we could not be registered. We were treated like second-class citizens in our country. Most of the NGO's turned us down. Those persons whose houses were totally destroyed received little to no help. It was hard and confusing going around in circles trying to get help. Thank God there were a few who helped us get the building back together. I thank God for His favor. We have so much to thank God for because He is truly taking care of us. We were able to have a place to live and to reopen the restaurant, which was a blessing. We were able to hire a few people and also help feed the people.

I am thankful to God for my granddaughter, who really followed in my footsteps. I turned the restaurant over to her after the hurricane. She packed grocery items to help other single moms and also gave them gift cards. I ended up working for her because we had to start all over with nothing. In spite of all the hard times, we never lost our faith. We stayed connected to God. God will use the things that the enemy intended for bad and will turn them around for good.

When my husband had that stroke, I was disappointed and hurt because I said to God this man preached the gospel on the streets for years. We went from one end of the island to the next, but we have to always follow the process. God will not allow the enemy to destroy us. My neighbors told me when the tornado hit our home, it was like a bomb went off. We had about eight feet of water in our home. If we were home, we would have all died. In all things, God is so faithful.

All of us have something to go through. We just have to trust God as we go through it. Sometimes it seems like we are forgotten on this journey. Many times we feel like the disciples when the storm was raging. Jesus was on the boat with them, but they couldn't understand how He could be sleeping at that time.

They asked Him if He didn't care that they were perishing. Jesus couldn't understand that the disciples didn't get it. The all-powerful One was on the boat with them. We are just like the disciples when the storms of life arise. We forget that Jesus is with us. He still calms the storm and gives us peace when we are going through it. Our faith in God will take us through anything. He will cause mountains to move out of your way. Jesus told them if they had the smallest faith, they could speak to the mountain and it would have to obey them. It's the same for us. Whatever is standing in your way, speak to it and it will have to move. We are connected to the Man who walked on water. He raised the dead and spoke to the winds and the waves and they had to obey Him. That same Jesus lives inside of us, and we have that same power. We just have to believe it. My journey was a hard one, but God brought me through because faith still works every time.

Conclusion

Jesus promised that He would take care of us. He reminded His disciples that He cared about the lilies of the field and the birds of the air. How much more will He care for us and meet every need? Sometimes it looks like there is no way out, but God always comes through. He doesn't want us to worry about anything. He wants us to build a relationship with Him as a Father. He wants us to trust and depend upon Him.

If you are sick, remember His words that by the stripes of Jesus, we are healed, and that's an assurance we can count on. His words will never change, and He assured us that healing is the bread for His children. Our healing comes not because we are Christians but because we have faith to believe.

Faith is a part of the armor that God has given us,

and when we put on the armor of God, we are fully protected. The Bible says that our shield of faith will quench every fiery dart that the enemy launches at us. Faith is not an option, because without it, you can't please God. It is not a garment that you put on and take off but a lifestyle.

Situations and circumstances are not supposed to shake our faith in God. He will keep us when the storms of life surround us. We will have peace because we know that He is in the storm with us. Daniel was not afraid of the lion's den because he had faith in the God that he served. The three Hebrew boys didn't let the fiery furnace shake their faith in God. When trouble comes, use the weapon that God has given you. Whatever you need from God, use the currency of heaven. Your faith will get you what you need.

About the Author

Lovely Reckley truly lives up to her name Lovely. She demonstrates a character of love and godliness. To her husband and family, she is a virtuous woman. One who is caring for the less fortunate and a voice agitating against the evil and injustice in society.

Made in the USA
Columbia, SC
23 November 2024